BRITAIN IN OLD

WEYMOUTH &

PORTLAND

TED GOSLING

ALAN SUTTON PUBLISHING LIMITED

Alan Sutton Publishing Limited
Phoenix Mill · Far Thrupp · Stroud
Gloucestershire · GL5 2BU

First published 1995

Cover photographs: (front) The Esplanade,
Weymouth; (back) Weymouth, c. 1879.

British Library Cataloguing in Publication Data.
A catalogue record for this book is available from
the British Library.

ISBN 0–7509–1140–9

Typeset in 9/10 Sabon.
Typesetting and origination by
Alan Sutton Publishing Limited.
Printed in Great Britain by
Ebenezer Baylis, Worcester.

Delighted children gather on the old Town Bridge to have their picture taken, c. 1909. Holy Trinity Church in the background was built in 1836 on a site facing the harbour. The church, a building of stone in the Perpendicular style, was restored and enlarged in 1887 and contains a pulpit of alabaster, presented in 1905 as a memorial to Hugh Speke.

Contents

A fine aerial picture of Weymouth, Portland and Portland Harbour. Thomas Hardy's Isle of Slingers from above looks like a bird's beak, and this view shows plainly the narrow strip of land that joins it to the mainland. The breakwater seen here forms one of the largest harbours in the world; it took twenty-three years to construct and cost the lives of twenty-four men. The final stone was laid by the Prince of Wales on 18 August 1872. Most of the construction was carried out by convicts, who had cut 5 million tons of stone to form the breakwater. The harbour was once the base for the Channel Fleet and until recent years was a crowded harbour filled with battleships, cruisers and destroyers.

Introduction

Weymouth owes its existence as a seaside resort to royal patronage. George III is reputed to have used the first bathing machine here in 1789, and when he emerged from it to go swimming in the bay a concealed band struck up 'God Save the King'. Today a statue of King George presides over one end of the long seafront with one of Queen Victoria at the other.

Weymouth has a wonderful curved bay which has been compared with the Bay of Naples. During the summer season it is a thriving seaside resort, but out of season the Georgian fronts and bow windows come into their own. Behind the seafront is the inner harbour, thick with small craft of every description. Beyond is Radipole Lake which is famous for its swans.

The small River Wey flows quietly into the sea and along both its banks are the piers, quays, warehouses and sidings that form the port of Weymouth. The Town Bridge, constructed of Portland stone, connects the two old parts of the town, and replaced an old wooden bridge which had seventeen arches. As a port Weymouth has a long history, having been granted its first charter in 1252. It was through the port that the Black Death first came to England in August 1348, with disastrous consequences for the whole country, killing two out of every five people. Weymouth supplied ships for Edward III against Calais and later more ships against the Spanish Armada, when two prize vessels were brought into the harbour. In an old house near the quay a cannon ball is embedded in the wall, a relic of the siege of Weymouth in the Civil War.

The quay is an old and interesting port, full of the flavour of shipping, with the public houses having a nautical air. Weymouth prospered and became a busy port, especially with the Channel Islands trade. Its success came about when the two towns of Weymouth and Melcombe Regis, on either side of the river, became a joint town with their amalgamation in 1571. The ridge called the Nothe, to the west of the town, has always been the guardian of the town, and today you can still visit the grey-walled fortress there.

The Isle of Portland is not far from the town and on the way to it is Wyke Regis, built on a hill, whose church was once the mother church for Weymouth. The two extensive churchyards around it are crammed with tombstones, many of them commemorating those who perished in wrecks in Deadman's Bay. Some of these were smugglers, and it is no coincidence that the Revenue Service had its base here.

Sir James Thornhill, the artist who decorated the dome of St Paul's Cathedral and many royal palaces, came from Weymouth and succeeded Sir Christopher Wren as MP for the town. Francis Bacon was MP for Melcombe Regis.

It is against this background that Ted Gosling has assembled a fine collection of old photographs which provides a valuable pictorial record for all those who are interested in old Weymouth and its port. It is the latest addition to the increasing series of his pictorial books covering the seaboard of both Dorset and Devon.

Roy F. Chapple
October 1995

The Channel Islands boat arrives at Weymouth, *c.* 1910. A typical quayside scene with a GWR train awaiting passengers.

All the hustle and bustle of a busy harbour is captured in this picture of Edwardian Weymouth taken by W. Pouncy, *c.* 1905. Cosens' paddle steamers the *Queen* and the *Albert Victor* can be seen in the harbour.

Section One

WEYMOUTH
THE EARLY DAYS

A Francis Frith photograph of the southern part of The Esplanade. The Nothe fort can be
clearly seen on the headland at the harbour entrance.

This print of Weymouth and the bay was published by the *Southern Times*, *c.* 1855. To give it its full title, the *Southern Times Dorsetshire Herald and Weymouth and Portland Gazette* was a local weekly paper. At the time of this print the paper, which was first published on 28 May 1851, had 16 pages and cost 3*d.*

The Jubilee Memorial Clock on the Weymouth Esplanade, pictured here in 1891, stands on an iron pedestal shaft some 44 ft in height. It was a gift to the town by Sir Henry Edwards MP to commemorate Queen Victoria's Golden Jubilee in 1887.

The Esplanade, north end, with St John's Church in the background, 1891. The lamp standards indicate that street lighting was provided by the Weymouth Gas Consumers' Company Limited.

Weymouth Esplanade and beach, *c*. 1855. The strong interest in local history which has developed in recent years has made photographs like this highly collectable. The photographer was clearly accomplished, and left behind this exceptionally fine picture of how Weymouth looked 140 years ago.

An early view of the Royal Terrace by Frith & Co., showing a quiet deserted Esplanade, 1880.

The photographer from Francis Frith & Co., who took this picture of The Esplanade and beach at Weymouth in 1903, succeeded in capturing the essence of that Edwardian summer day long ago. It was a time when the sun shone uninterruptedly from a blue sky; a carefree time when people made their own amusements and seemingly enjoyed them all the more. Looking at this picture of a crowded beach with horse buses carrying people, we can see that little has changed in this Weymouth landscape of some ninety years ago.

View across the backwater showing the old Westham Bridge, *c.* 1904. This bridge was replaced later with the Westham Bridge of today.

Backwater Bridge (old Westham Bridge) with Melcombe Regis railway bridge in the background, *c.* 1900. The wooden railway bridge for the Weymouth and Portland railway was built in 1862.

The Church of St Mary, Melcombe Regis, 1903. The clock in the tower with the cupola was installed in 1894.

St Mary Street, *c*. 1905. Note the rear of the Royal Baths on the right-hand side.

Weymouth Harbour, 1884. This fine picture of the harbour over 100 years ago shows a very peaceful scene.

Weymouth Esplanade and beach, *c.* 1910.

The Esplanade and beach, 1890. Note The Royal Dorset Yacht Club with the flag-pole. The Club was formed in 1875 and was later granted permission by the Admiralty to fly the Blue Ensign of His Majesty's Fleet.

Postcard from Weymouth, *c.* 1898. This was the heyday of the picture postcard. Plain postcards appeared in 1870, and by 1880 the first of those bearing pictures became available. Everyone on holiday sent cards back home and today seaside postcards like this have a special place in the collector's heart.

Waterloo Place with St John's Church in the background, *c.* 1897. St John's, a building of stone in the Gothic style, was opened in 1854 to serve the growing population of the area as it expanded northwards. At the date of this picture the vicar was Canon John Stephenson, and the church holds a memorial brass to commemorate his long period of service, 1854–1905.

Weymouth beach, 1895. This was a popular haunt of holiday-makers during the second half of the nineteenth century.

A fine picture of the harbour from the drawbridge, *c.* 1890. It shows a busy scene with sailing vessels and coasters unloading in the harbour.

View from the backwater looking towards Rodwell, 1890.

The pier and Esplanade with the bay in the background, c. 1891. The two paddle steamers seen in this picture were the *Queen* and the *Victoria*, which were operated by Cosens & Co. Ltd.

The statue of George III (on the right) is seen here in 1895 with St Thomas and St Mary streets behind the statue running westward towards the harbour (see also pp. 45, 46).

Weymouth Harbour, *c*. 1887. A fine study of sail in the harbour of 100 years ago.

The GWR Weymouth to Cherbourg paddle steamer *Gael* swinging into the cove. The small steamer on the left appears to be Messrs Cosens' *Prince*, but the one on the right has not been identified. *Gael* was only on the Cherbourg service from April 1884 until January 1885 and this photograph is the only known one to be taken of her in Weymouth Harbour. The trees in the background are still in leaf, which suggests that the photograph was taken in the summer of 1884.

The entrance to Weymouth Harbour between the pier and the Nothe, *c.* 1890. The paddle steamer seen in the picture is the *Queen*, one of the Cosens' fleet.

The sea, boats and ships are always a fascinating sight to watch, and pictured here we see boats of every description entering and leaving Weymouth Harbour, 1888.

Dorchester Road, Weymouth, 1898. Modern motor traffic may have brought many advantages to our community, but at what cost? Dorchester Road was then a peaceful highway where people could stop and chat with no fear of being knocked down.

Weymouth College was founded in 1863 and controlled by the Evangelical Church Schools. These men are working on the new College Chapel, c. 1895. The foundation stone of this chapel was laid by the Lord Bishop of Salisbury on 13 June 1895.

Originally known as Weymouth Grammar School, Weymouth College in Dorchester Road is seen here in 1895. Weymouth College closed in 1939 and is now part of Dorset Institute of Higher Education.

Weymouth College from the east, 16 June 1895. Weymouth College stood in grounds of some 20 acres.

St Mary Street, from the corner of Bond Street, looking north, c. 1901. Taken before the Midland Bank was built on the site of Messrs Williams, draper's, you can see from the lamp standard on the right that the street lighting was provided by the gas company.

Victoria Terrace and the Burdon Hotel, c. 1879 (see also p. 42). Completed in 1855, Victoria Terrace was at first occupied by private residents. The Burdon Hotel is now named the Prince Regent, and during the First World War was used as a hospital for wounded servicemen.

St Thomas Street, Weymouth, *c.* 1900.

Sandsfoot Castle. Further along the cliffs from the Nothe are the ruins of Sandsfoot Castle, which was erected in 1553 by Henry VIII to protect Portland Roads.

The GWR Weymouth to Cherbourg paddle steamer *Great Western*, berthed at the original wooden cargo stage at Weymouth Harbour. This steamer arrived at Weymouth for the opening of the Cherbourg service on 1 August 1878 and remained in use until the service closed on 30 June 1885. The railway wagons mark the end of the harbour tramway as it was from its opening in October 1865 until the early part of 1880. Both the tramway and the cargo stage were then extended. This photograph may therefore be dated to 1878 or 1879. The 1880 extension of the tramway was followed in 1889 by a more important extension with the introduction of passenger trains to the quay.

The expansion of the railway network made it easy for the Victorians to travel to the coast and spend their holidays in resorts like Weymouth. Views such as this one of Weymouth Esplanade and the beach, taken in 1885 by Francis Frith & Co., were bought by visitors as souvenirs of their holiday and sent to their friends at home.

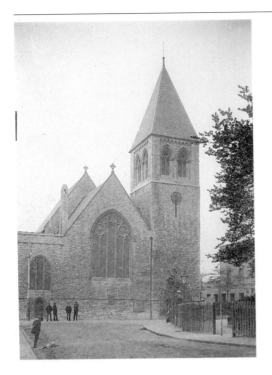

Christ Church, Melcombe Regis, erected in 1874, is pictured here in about 1900. The clock in the tower was the gift of Sir Henry Edwards.

Weymouth's old railway station in King Street, now demolished, in a view from 1913, was the joint station of the Great Western and Southern Railways. The corner of the Somerset Inn can be seen on the right.

The paddle steamers *Aquila* and *Cygnus* were built in 1854 by Jas Henderson & Son of Renfrew. They were not identical but for practical purposes sister ships, and were very hard to tell apart. The one pictured here is almost certainly the *Aquila*: the evidence is not absolutely conclusive but all that there is, including comparison with other photographs, suggests this.

Aquila and *Cygnus* started a service between Harwich and Antwerp for the North of Europe Steam Navigation Co., the *Aquila* on 23 September 1854, and the *Cygnus* shortly afterwards. The service was not a success and by 1857, when the newly formed Weymouth & Channel Islands Steam Packet Co. was in the market for ships, both the *Aquila* and the *Cygnus* were laid up at Victoria Dock, London. They were taken on charter by the Channel Islands Company with effect from 13 April and started the new service on 17 April, the *Cygnus* were from Weymouth and the *Aquila* from Jersey.

They were bought outright in October 1857 but for much of the time between then and June 1889, when the service was taken over by the Great Western Railway, they were on mortgage, the Channel Islands Company being chronically in the red and kept going only by financial support of various kinds from the GWR, by agreement with whom the service was conducted. Both ships were fitted with oscillating engines by McNabb & Clark of Greenock, which gave them a speed of about 12 knots.

The wagons in the background mark the end of the harbour tramway as it was from the date of opening, October 1865, until the GWR introduced passenger trains direct to the pier and extended the tramway to the baggage shed for that purpose. Various details date the photograph as having been taken between August 1878 and early 1880.

St Mary Street from Bond Street corner, *c.* 1900.

Print of the original Weymouth College building.

A Francis Frith & Co. picture of The Esplanade and the Royal Terrace, *c.* 1885. In this photograph people are standing in the middle of the road!

The old Town Bridge, c. 1925.

Looking towards the Nothe with Weymouth Pavilion in the background, c. 1910. In the foreground, outside the Alexandra Gardens, the statue of Sir Henry Edwards was erected by public subscription in 1885. Sir Henry Edwards was Weymouth's MP from 1867 till 1885, when the town ceased to be a parliamentary borough. Weymouth benefited from his many generous gifts, including the Jubilee Clock. Note the fine Edwardian motor-cars on the Parade.

Section Two

THE TOWN

The back of Christ Church can be seen on the left of this picture. Christ Church, which stood at the King Street/Park Street junction, was demolished in the 1950s.

Nos 11–12 Clarence Buildings, *c.* 1938.

Hurdle's shop, a Tudor house in Maiden Street, just before demolition in 1922.

The St Thomas street entrance to the Royal Baths, not long before the building was demolished in 1927. The Royal Baths were built in 1842 but by the time of this picture were used mainly as offices. Note the premises of the South Dorset Liberal Association on the right.

The Tudor house, Braemar, North Quay, 1937. This building became a victim of progress when it was demolished in the 1960s along with other properties to make room for the new municipal offices.

Westham Road photographed by R.J. Smart, 1938. The shops seen here were demolished not long after this picture was taken, and a new block built.

Johnson Row was built in the early part of the nineteenth century, and is seen here in 1939.

26–8 Trinity Street, *c.* 1936. When this picture was taken Chas Hayman the hairdresser occupied No. 26, and could the shop with J.S. Oliver displayed over the entrance have been the home of Joseph Sidney Oliver, the local fishmonger?

Another example of a photograph rich in information about pre-war Weymouth. Taken in 1938 it pictures the back of a house at the north-east of Trinity Street.

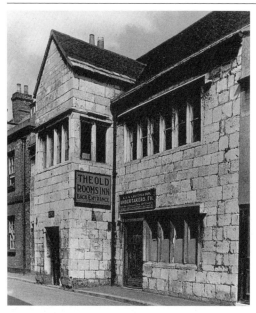

The Old Rooms Inn, Trinity Street, Weymouth, 1938.

This fine photograph of Trinity Street with the Old Rooms Inn in the background was taken by V.F.M. Oliver in 1937.

This V.F.M. Oliver photograph shows the Tudor house in Trinity Street, 1937.

The Park Street side of the Gloucester Street Congregational Church, founded in 1658, although the church pictured here was built in 1864 from designs by Mr R.C. Bennett. The church was last used for regular worship in 1971, and was demolished in 1980.

The Gloucester Street Congregational
Church looking towards The Esplanade,
taken by Mr A.T. Walker, May 1971.
The church was built in the
Romanesque style with a tower 190 ft
high.

The interior of Gloucester Street Congregational Church, 1971.

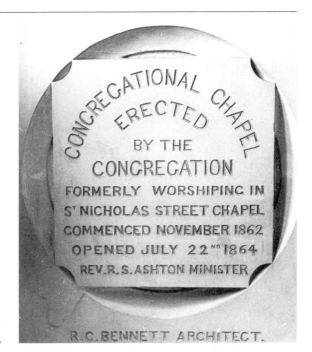

The stone plaque commemorating the opening of the Gloucester Street Congregational Church. This plaque was inside the church.

Gloucester Street Congregational Church was last used for regular worship in 1971, and demolition of the building took place in 1980. This fine picture of the interior, viewed from the choir stalls, was taken in 1971 by Mr A.T. Walker. Photographs like this, dated and fully annotated by the photographer, become an important source of information for local historians.

These pictures of Brunswick Terrace, taken in 1939 by V.F.M. Oliver, are fine examples of documentary photography, showing the pre-war architecture of Weymouth. Brunswick Terrace, once known as Brunswick Buildings, was built in 1827.

This interesting architectural photograph shows the stone framework and the door to the end house of Royal Terrace.

The end house, Royal Terrace.

Victoria Terrace and the Burdon Hotel, *c.* 1938. Victoria Terrace was the final terrace to be built on The Esplanade and with the Burdon Hotel was completed in 1855.

The Royal Terrace and the Gloucester Hotel, *c.* 1965.

The Royal Terrace showing modern alterations, c. 1965. Weymouth first became famous as a seaside resort when George III visited the town, and by the time of this picture was still a favourite and delightful place for families to come for their annual holiday.

Completed in the 1850s, Belvedere Terrace is pictured here in 1938.

The Gloucester Hotel, *c.* 1938. Built in the eighteenth century as a summer residence for the Duke of Gloucester, the then Gloucester Lodge (or the Royal Lodge as it became known) was home to George III during his holiday visits to Weymouth. The left-hand section of the building was added in the 1860s as The Country Club, later becoming a part of the hotel.

Another pre-war photograph by V.F.M. Oliver, 1938. This one shows the houses between the Gloucester and Royal Hotels, showing the original buildings with modern alterations in Gloucester Row.

This pre-war picture shows the elegant Fountain Hotel in King Street, occupied today by the bookmakers Coral.

Our ancestors were great ones for erecting statues. This striking photograph of the life-size statue of George III reminds passers-by of his patronage of the town (see p. 18).

Standing proud at the top of St Mary Street is the statue of George III, erected in 1810 to commemorate the fiftieth year of his reign. The picture dates from about 1938.

The noble lion which sits at the base of the statue of George III.

Another fine architectural picture by V.F.M. Oliver, showing the house at the corner of South Parade and the quay, 1938.

The Golden Lion Hotel, St Edmund Street, *c.* 1929. At the time of this photograph the hotel was under the ownership of Mr W.R. Prudon. He advertised the business as a 'Family and Commercial' hotel, and allowed the Weymouth Football Club to use it as their headquarters.

Another fine photograph by V.F.M. Oliver, showing the architecture of Weymouth. Here we see houses in Charlotte Row, adjoining the Yacht Club, c. 1938.

4A York Buildings, taken by V.F.M. Oliver, c. 1939. York Buildings, completed in 1783, was the first terrace facing the sea to be built in the town.

King Street from The Esplanade, with the Fountain Hotel on the left.

The Theatre Royal at the lower end of St Nicholas Street opened in 1865 in converted chapel buildings. Seen here in 1930 are the doorway and entrance arch. The theatre was demolished in 1968.

The old Town Bridge, Weymouth, *c*. 1925.

The Town Bridge was built between 1928 and 1930 when the old stone bridge in the picture above was dismantled. During the construction of the new bridge, shown here in 1929, a temporary wooden bridge was erected for pedestrians. The new Town Bridge was opened by HRH the Duke of York on 4 July 1930.

The old Town Bridge is pictured here before it was rebuilt in 1929. The stones from this bridge were bought by Sir Ernest Debenham of Moore Lane House, Briantspuddle, to build the Briantspuddle Bridge.

The Town Bridge, pictured here not long after the official opening, *c.* 1931. The two-arm control opening is in operation; this allowed entry for larger ships.

The Market House, St Mary Street, *c.* 1910. The Market House was opened in 1855 and at the time of this picture the market was held daily, with special days on Tuesdays and Fridays. Note the Tudor dormer on the right-hand side of the photograph.

The Market House. The building survived until 1939 when it was demolished. One end wall facing the churchyard is still standing.

No. 6 Hope Street, taken in about 1938 by V.F.M. Oliver.

Another picture by V.F.M. Oliver. It shows the Georgian houses in the east end of Westham Road just before their demolition in 1939.

Nos 1–2 York Buildings on
Weymouth Esplanade, c. 1939.

General view of Weymouth, with The Esplanade in the background, 1890.

Belfield House, *c.* 1900. This elegant mansion was designed for the Buxton family by John Crunden, *c.* 1778.

Weymouth Hospital, 1903.

Waterloo Place was built in 1835. This picture was taken in 1938 by V.F.M. Oliver.

Almshouses in Wyke Road, taken by V.F.M. Oliver, 1936. These almshouses, which were erected in the early nineteenth century, were demolished in 1957.

Section Three

BESIDE THE
SEASIDE

The Esplanade, c. 1923. During the 1920s a day spent by the sea at Weymouth could be quiet or boisterous, depending on taste. For the people in this picture the promenade was the place to stroll – or sit and watch for the latest fashions.

This fine early aerial picture of The Esplanade and beach was taken at the height of the summer season. The beach is crowded with holiday-makers and day-trippers. For them, as for present-day visitors to Weymouth, there were many delights to please old and young alike. The beach provided plenty of entertainment with donkey rides, Punch and Judy shows and swings. Then as now the excited shrieks of children could be heard as they enjoyed themselves.

Weymouth beach and Esplanade, *c.* 1903. The noise must have been astonishing, with minstrels, Punch and Judy shows, brass bands, hurdy-gurdy men and barrel organs all vying for attention.

Yachts at anchor beside the Nothe, *c.* 1910.

Weymouth Esplanade, summer 1918. For the women pictured here it was a time of unrest. The war had lasted too long with appalling loss of life, and with husbands absent at the front the worry for them must have been overwhelming.

Weymouth beach, c. 1906. The bathing machine shown in this photograph was reputed to be the one used by George III during his visits to the town. There is a story told to the effect that when King George made his first plunge into the sea he was saluted from a neighbouring bathing machine with the strains of 'God Save the King'.

Bathing machines, Weymouth beach, *c.* 1894. These bathing machines had two compartments, a 'dry' section for disrobing and a 'wet' one for putting on the costumes. The machine was pushed down to the sea until the wheels were half-submerged; the ladies then went down three steps to stand in the sea.

Weymouth Parade, 1898. Frith's photographer has successfully captured much detail here. The people dressed in black, the children building sand-castles with their hats on, the horse-drawn carriages lined up on the parade, flags fluttering, all combine to give a picture of great visual interest.

Weymouth Esplanade and beach, 1944. The resort in wartime, with landing craft to be used on D-day lying on the beach.

The Bungalows and Greenhill beach, 1925.

A busy summer day on The Esplanade and beach, summer 1898.

The Alexandra Gardens and Esplanade, *c.* 1898. In the late nineteenth century, seaside resorts such as Weymouth owed their popularity to the variety of entertainment they could provide. The bandstand pictured here was erected in 1891 and was much used by visiting bands and orchestras.

Weymouth sands, *c.* 1890. There is a magic, a degree of vividness about this picture which the photographer from Francis Frith & Co. managed to capture. The seaside holiday was a special treat for children. They were given the chance to run about in the open air, jump on the beach and experience the delight of a first paddle in the sea. This enchanting picture of a century ago enables us to share the happiness of that summer day.

Ferryboats, *c*. 1970. These ferryboats were continuing a long tradition of such vessels stretching back to the early days of the nineteenth century. The ferry service between the Channel Islands and Weymouth has always played an important part in the ports' activities, with the Condor hydrofoils of the present day still maintaining the service.

This fine view of Alexandra Gardens was taken by Francis Frith & Co. in 1923. The building seen here was a glass structure known as the Kursaal, built in 1913 to protect the bandstand and audience from the rain. The building was demolished not long after this picture was taken, to be replaced in 1924 with the Alexandra Garden Theatre.

The harbour and bay by Francis Frith & Co, 1891.

The Esplanade with the Pavilion in the background, *c.* 1909. Another gem from Francis Frith & Co., picturing an early motor-car. Certainly there was more space for parking in those days!

The Esplanade and beach, *c.* 1905. The bathing machines pictured here were used by the ladies who were keen to preserve their modesty. In those days getting a tan certainly was not fashionable, and most people wore their Sunday best on the beach.

Weymouth sands, July 1914. Despite the seriousness of the international situation few of the people pictured here enjoying their holiday at Weymouth realized that this was the last of those golden Edwardian summers. They could hardly have guessed that it would be five long years before Weymouth would enjoy a summer in peace.

The Esplanade and sands, 1923. After the First World War, like many resorts, Weymouth enjoyed a boom period, catering for visitors who had not been able to come during the difficult days of the war.

A beach scene at Weymouth, c. 1900.

Weymouth sands, c. 1899. A ride across the sands on a docile donkey delighted children and adults alike. The Downton family provided donkeys for the visitors and are still doing so today. One old Weymouth wag of that period when asked 'How do you hire a donkey?' would always reply, 'Put a screw beneath the saddle'.

The Esplanade and Parade, 1923. The seaside holiday became firmly established in the Victorian age, and by the 1920s railway and coach travel had made it possible for the majority of people to visit resorts like Weymouth. The Esplanade fronting the sea, with benches and seats placed at convenient intervals, was then as now a favourite place to stroll or sit and watch the world go by. Weymouth had many attractions to entertain visitors, and away from the beach firms like the Weymouth Motor Company Limited ran motor-coach trips to all the local places of interest.

The Esplanade, north end, 1903. A typical Edwardian seaside picture.

A typical summer snapshot from Weymouth, *c.* 1919. This was a time after the long war years when people were beginning to rediscover the country and especially the seaside. The holiday-makers pictured here on a summer afternoon must have been glad to have survived the turbulent times of the First World War and are relaxing in the warm sun.

This picture, taken in 1909, shows the first Pavilion Theatre which was built at Weymouth in 1908 at a cost of £13,000. The main part of the building was used as a theatre, and in addition there was a skating rink and dining rooms. For nearly fifty years this theatre, later renamed the Ritz, was the venue for summer shows until it was destroyed by fire on 13 April 1954. The new theatre which replaced it opened in 1960.

Section Four

JUST PEOPLE

This group of happy young cyclists are ready to ride off, outside St Mary's Church, 1958.

Insofar as any group in a community can impose an image on an age, for Victorian England that group was the middle class. Weymouth residents Emma Elizabeth Burtt, left, who died on 10 October 1956, and her sister Agnes Annie, below, were members of that class. In the last years of the nineteenth century they posed for these pictures, to be added to that enduring feature of the Victorian home, the leather-bound family photograph album, which was usually fastened with a brass clasp. Their images survive, showing that although the fashions of this period had practical drawbacks they offered grace to those who were able to wear them to advantage.

Weymouth resident Edith Sarah Burtt, who died on 21 January 1956, is pictured here in the late nineteenth century. We are left with the image of a flawless face with the enigmatic smile of a Mona Lisa, captured exquisitely by Wayland, the Victorian photographer.

Gloucester Street, Weymouth, Church Choir, c. 1905. Members of the choir include William Cornish (front row, first left), who was born in 1865 and had a baker's shop in East Street; William Surtees (front row, centre), who was born in 1872, worked at Whiteheads and died in 1957; Mr Milledge (back row, second from the right), who was an auctioneer; Mr Brown (back row, fourth from the left), who also worked at Whiteheads; William Dawes (back row, seventh from the left).

Tea on the terrace at 29 Melcombe Avenue, 1932. Pictured, left to right: Charles Falkner, Ann Falkner, Mrs C. Falkner and Peter Mead.

A delightful family photograph of the Falkners of Weymouth, *c.* 1929. Left to right: Drusilla, Elizabeth, Mrs Falkner, Thomas, Christiana and John.

Weymouth beach, *c.* 1921. For those who could afford a seaside holiday, paddling with their children away from workaday cares was one of the activities they enjoyed.

Mr Charles Falkner of Melcombe Avenue is pictured here on Greenhill beach carrying buckets and spades to make sand-castles with Elizabeth Falkner, 1929.

Until the 1950s a novelty available for the children of visitors was a ride in a goat carriage. The goats were harnessed in pairs and led by a young boy who drew the carriage along The Esplanade and across the sands.

A ride in the goat carriage at Weymouth.

A day of warm hazy sunshine with members of the Falkner family enjoying a day on the beach at Weymouth, *c.* 1929. Here we see, left to right: ? Wilkinson, ? Binghams, Drue Falkner, Ruth Halls and Elizabeth Falkner.

Photographs like this of family groups on Weymouth beach taken in the 1920s evoke a nostalgia for a vanished state of society. It was a time when the middle classes set the example for others. It was a time of innocence before the years of depression and war of the 1930s and '40s changed the face of England for ever.

Greenhill beach, Weymouth, *c.* 1929. Between the two world wars seaside resorts enjoyed an increasing popularity. Here we see, left to right, Elizabeth Porode, Mrs Charles Falkner and Phyllis Western. The low-slung canvas and wooden deckchairs pictured were essential for comfort on the beach.

By the 1920s women's bathing dresses had become less elaborate. In this picture we can see Miss Drusilla Falkner bathing in the sea at Weymouth during the summer of 1925, wearing a costume typical of the period.

Mrs Charles Falkner faces the camera for this delightful picture taken in the garden of 29 Melcombe Avenue. The lady with her back to the photographer was Drusilla Falkner.

Smart coats and shoes, and smiles all round, make this a really happy picture of a walk along the Weymouth Parade, c. 1929. The ladies are, left to right: Mrs Halls, Ruth Halls, Marjorie Tyrrell, Kathleen Vidler and Christiana Falkner.

The Richardson family visiting Weymouth on a day trip, 1928. Sisters Elizabeth and Emily, sitting on the sand, are wearing clothes typical of the period: the cloche hat, the more daring beret, dresses designed to flatten the figure, twenties-look shoes. This was the look that gave the name of 'flapper' to the 'bright young things'.

Weymouth beach, summer 1904. By the beginning of the twentieth century the seaside holiday had become an annual event for all who could afford it. For the children an integral part of such holidays was the opportunity to ride across the sands on a donkey.

The summer of 1929 must have had some warm nights because pictured here we see a member of the Falkner family sleeping on the terrace of 29 Melcombe Avenue.

This picture is unique in showing a group of Weymouth men who were born in the eighteenth century. Peter Green, pictured in the centre of the group, served with Nelson on the *Victory* at Trafalgar in 1805 and was probably born at about the time of the French Revolution. The original photograph of about 1855, which was in the Weymouth boatman's shelter, was stolen by an Australian soldier during the First World War.

This photograph was taken at Weymouth. The driver of the bus was Ivor House who operated from Milton, with trips to Dorchester and Weymouth. The passengers include Mrs Peerman, Granny Tucker and, on the extreme right in the foreground, seven-year-old Charles Humber.

A charming picture of a Saunders family event. The occasion is unknown, but judging by the couple in the middle it could have been a family wedding.

Section Five

IN TIME OF WAR

Many brave men from the United States Army left Weymouth and Portland for the invasion

of Normandy on 6 June 1944. The part they played is commemorated in a memorial

erected on Weymouth Esplanade opposite the Royal Hotel. In this picture, taken on a grey

day in December 1947, the unveiling ceremony of the D-day Memorial is taking place.

Portland, June 1944. The embarkation of American troops is pictured en route for the invasion of France.

Submarine H43 pictured in Weymouth bay, 19 July 1935.

American landing craft gathered in Portland Harbour before the Normandy landings, June 1944. 'Operation Overlord' was the greatest seaborne invasion in military history. In a single day some 176,000 men went ashore, together with 3,000 guns, 1,500 tanks and 15,000 assorted military vehicles. D-day was to become one of the most evocative words of this century, with Portland and Weymouth playing an important part as loading ports.

By the summer of 1939 Britain was becoming prepared to fight and the illusions of the 1930s were fast disappearing. Conscription came in on 1 July and here in August, just before the outbreak of war, we see the Royal Engineers at Portland taking target practice.

The dedication ceremony of the Portland War Memorial, 1920s. Monuments like this were erected in every town and village of the country, with the names of those who had died carved in stone as a lasting remembrance of their final sacrifice. For the people of Portland it was a day of pride, but for the mothers and fathers, the wives and children who knew their loved ones would never return, it must have been a day of deep sorrow.

Members of Weymouth's wartime St John Ambulance Brigade alongside 'Khaki', the ambulance which was presented to them by the American Red Cross in 1940. Left to right: Pte Bennett, Miss L. Baille, Mrs Groves (the Red Cross Commandant), Mrs Bartlett (the Lady Superintendent of the St John Ambulance Brigade) and Lt/Cpl Haines.

Pictured here during June 1944 are US troops marching along Weymouth Esplanade en route for embarkation to Normandy.

Shown here in 1944 three months before D-day is a Humber armoured car being driven down the ramp of an LCT (tank landing craft) into Weymouth Bay.

American amphibious armour in Weymouth Bay, 1944. Note Weymouth's anti-invasion bay defences in the background.

Pictured here is a Swordfish biplane taking off from an experimental floating airfield, which was being tried out in Weymouth Bay, 1944. The Navy Swordfish was a torpedo bomber which was used during the Second World War for both slow and low flying. It is estimated, however, that 95 per cent of the crews were lost in action.

The Fleet, Portland, *c.* 1910. This demonstration of our first line of defence was at a time when the sovereignty of the Royal Navy was far-reaching and absolute, with a harbour like Portland providing shelter for British warships. Although the Royal Navy was still the most powerful maritime force in the world when Edward VII ascended the throne, apathy, poor ship design and old ideas put it under threat from the new naval power of Germany. The restless energy of Admiral Sir John Arbuthnot Fisher, who became the First Sea Lord in 1904, brought the navy into the twentieth century, and by the time of this picture they were ready for modern war.

HMS *Formidable*, pictured here at Portland in 1914, was launched on 17 November 1898. On that date she carried the most powerful guns in existence and was regarded as unsinkable. Unfortunately not long after this photograph was taken, this pre-war Dreadnought was sunk. It was on New Year's Day 1915 that she was struck by a torpedo some miles off the Devon coast and because of the rough seas and intense cold weather there were only about 200 survivors out of a complement of 790 officers and men.

HMS *Hood* being manoeuvred into position across the southern entrance of Portland Harbour, November 1914. Later the *Hood* was sunk as an anti-submarine obstacle.

The first U-boat to reach a British port after Germany's unconditional surrender on 8 May 1945 was U249 pictured here entering Portland Harbour.

Strip cultivation in the open fields of Portland.

The Channel Fleet at Portland, *c.* 1909.

Section Six

HIGH DAYS AND
EVENTS

Sweethill Lane, Portland, during the floods of
October–November 1960.

Greenhill Bowling Green, *c.* 1930.

The towers of Gloucester Street Congregational Church viewed from the high ground above the station on a misty and windy day in 1971. This church suffered from subsidence and was later demolished.

Taking a large group photograph is something of an art, and the photographer deserves congratulations for this picture of the 8th Competitive Choral Festival, held in Weymouth in about 1920, where everyone has been persuaded to look at the centre.

Crowds gather to see the ceremony of laying the foundation stone of Weymouth College Chapel by the Lord Bishop of Salisbury, 13 June 1895.

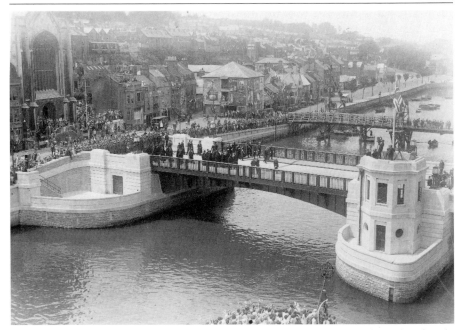

Crowds gather to watch the official opening of the Town Bridge by HRH the Duke of York, 4 July 1930. Special events such as this would have the local photographer on the spot with his camera. A careful examination of the right-hand tower of the bridge-top reveals the local press photographers gathered to obtain that important shot of the occasion.

With the advent of the motor-car came motor sport. Here in Weymouth during the early years of the century a meeting of the Dorset Automobile Club is taking place under the fascinated gaze of the onlookers.

The French schooner *Madeleine Tristan*, laden with grain, is pictured here near Chesil Cove, September 1930.

The *Madeleine Tristan* aground near Chesil Cove, September 1930.

The lighthouse on the Bill acts as a warning to shipping of the dangers that abound in Portland waters. Since the seventeenth century more than 400 shipwrecks have been recorded in this area. These two dramatic pictures show the paddle steamer *Bournemouth*, which went aground on Portland during the 1890s. They were taken by a photographer from Dorchester who must have had great difficulty in getting his bulky camera and photographic plates into position to take these pictures.

The Greek steamer *Prevexa* grounded on Chesil beach, January 1920.

The fire at 9, 10 and 11 Trinity Street, behind Trinity Church, *c.* 1924. The occupier of the house in which the fire started left the boiler on in the wash-house and went out, forgetting to put it out.

Christmas buffet lunch at the Royal Hotel, *c.* 1948. The chef pictured here in the middle wearing his big white hat and overalls is everyone's image of how a chef should look, and despite food rationing he has managed to provide a good spread.

'Happy Christmas', the Royal Hotel, *c.* 1948. After the war few people considered travelling abroad; indeed during the war many had been abroad and were grateful to be back home. Christmas breaks were then becoming popular and people were beginning to enjoy themselves again.

The Church Congress in Weymouth, 1905. This procession of clergy along The Esplanade attracted a large number of spectators. Religion played an important part in Edwardian daily life, with attendance essential at least once a week at some place of worship. The middle class or well-to-do would almost certainly have supported the Church of England, and processions like this became a social event not to be missed. Such meetings were held so that clergy could discuss their new and more active role in the community in the new century.

Weymouth Regatta, 1889. Yachting, or to use a humbler term sailing, is a magnificent sport which then as now attracted a special breed of person – an individualist with a great love of the sea.

St Thomas Street, Weymouth, *c.* 1905. This picture dates from before the destruction of the Royal Baths. The people on the pavement are gathering to see the arrival of Sanger's Circus. Visiting fairs and circuses were among the events that took place during the summer months and their arrival was looked forward to by enthusiastic spectators.

Section Seven

PORTLAND AND ITS PEOPLE

Portland and the Chesil beach, 1889. With Chesil beach running away in the background

this fine view of Chiswell and Portland Harbour was taken by Francis Frith. In his

History of Dorset, *John Hutchins said of the Portland people: 'They are a stout, hardy,*

industrious race, and in general better informed than most labouring people, very healthy

but not long-lived, for though at 60 many of the men appear strong and robust they soon

drop off, and there are no instances of great longevity, which may be accounted for from too

great a use of spirits.'

Chiswell Village and the Verne from Chesil beach, 1891. Note the old police house on the left in Castle Road.

Taken at the turn of the century this picture shows a procession passing through Fortuneswell.

A general view of Fortuneswell, 1890.

Sandsfoot Castle, *c.* 1910.

General view of Portland and the Chesil beach, *c.* 1900. The Chesil Bank, which stretches from Portland to Abbotsbury, is separated from the mainland by a narrow channel called the Fleet. This bank of pebbles about ten miles long resembles the curve of a scythe-blade, with stones which are automatically graded from west to east, becoming larger towards the Isle of Portland. As a result of this grading, local fog-bound fishermen can come ashore, pick up a stone and tell their exact location.

The gates of the convict prison, Grove, *c.* 1896. At the time of this photograph up to 1,500 prisoners were held in this establishment and, according to the records, these included MPs, bank directors, railway secretaries, cashiers of large firms and clergymen. If the warders of that time could come back today they would find many improvements, but the occupations of the inmates would be familiar to them.

The Castletown waterfront with Fort Verne in the background, 1891.

The old higher lighthouse at Portland Bill at the turn of the century. This building was replaced by the present lighthouse in 1906.

Grove Prison, *c.* 1910.

Portland Lighthouse, *c.* 1972.

Old houses at the entrance to Pennsylvania Castle, 1900. This castle was built for John Penn, whose grandfather was founder of the State of Pennsylvania, USA.

Fortuneswell, August 1878. On the left-hand side of this photograph you can see a fine example of a fossilized tree, standing over 20 ft high against the house. This tree is now in the Dorset County Museum.

Portland Tudor Castle, pictured here from the landward side, 1938. Overlooking the harbour, Portland Castle was built in 1539 by Henry VIII. The castle saw much action during the Civil War, changing hands more than once. Today it is one of the best preserved of King Henry's castles. It is under the care of English Heritage and regularly open to the public.

The main road rising up through Fortuneswell, *c*. 1891.

Portland street scene by Francis Frith & Co. of Reigate. Frith, who was born in 1822, settled in Reigate and opened a photographic business there in 1860. With his associate photographers he produced hundreds of thousands of photographs of the British Isles, Europe and the Middle East. These mass-produced photographs of familiar places such as this one were sold as prints or postcards at a modest price.

A fine example of a traction engine hauling stone past Portland's Victoria Gardens, *c.* 1923.

Rufus Castle and the graveyard of St Andrew's Church, 1890. Rufus Castle, known locally as 'bow and arrow castle', was built in the fifteenth century to defend Church-ope-Cove against invaders from the sea. Both castle and church are now in ruins.

Portland Roads and breakwater, *c.* 1895. The ship seen here was HMS *Boscowen*, Portland's training ship. Within a few years vessels such as this would be replaced with new training schools, along with a new curriculum replacing the outdated syllabus.

THE BATH & PORTLAND STONE FIRMS, Limited,

PORTLAND AND BATH.

THE LARGEST QUARRY OWNERS ON THE ISLAND.

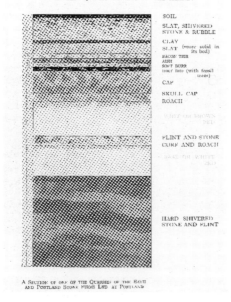

SOIL

SLAT, SHIVERED STONE & RUBBLE

CLAY
SLAT (more solid in its bed)
BACON TIER
AISH
SOFT BURR
DIRT BED (with fossil trees)

CAP

SKULL CAP
ROACH

WHIT OR BROWN BED

FLINT AND STONE
CURF AND ROACH

BASE OR WHITE BED

HARD SHIVERED STONE AND FLINT

A SECTION OF ONE OF THE QUARRIES OF THE BATH
AND PORTLAND STONE FIRMS LTD AT PORTLAND

Chart showing a section of quarry belonging to the Bath and Portland Stone Firms Ltd.

The quarrying of building stone in Portland formed the major industry there, and extensive use of it was made by Sir Christopher Wren. Wren's quarry mark seen here indicated that the architect needed the stones so marked.

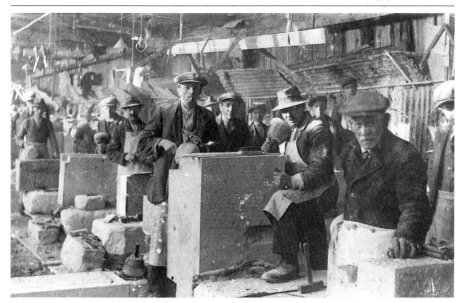

Inside F.J. Barnes' masonry shop at Wide Street, Portland, 1926. In the foreground holding mallets, left to right, are: Jimmy Durston, Tom Croad and Harry Hawkins.

The masonry yard belonging to the Bath and Portland Stone Firms Ltd, at the bottom of Coombe Park Road, *c.* 1950. The saw shown here in the main shop of no. 4 yard was installed after the Second World War.

The name Portland is synonymous with stone, and in London alone the majority of important buildings were built of stone taken from its quarries. The men working here in a Portland stone works are highly skilled craftsmen.

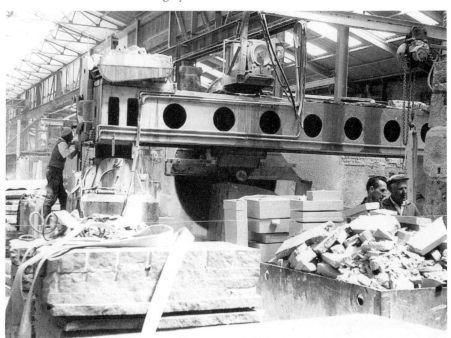

Interior of a Portland stone works with a giant saw slicing through the stone, 1965.

Lifting a large block of Portland stone by crane, summer 1966. This view was taken by David Willis.

Pictured here is a Portland quarryman drilling for blasting with a pneumatic drill, summer 1966. The top layer was blasted and then cleared away, and the best stone layer removed without blasting.

In this David Willis photograph a Portland quarryman is using a large sledge to drive in plugs and feathers, August 1966.

The quarryman seen here is driving in plugs and feathers to split the stone. The stone would then be squared up using kivels, before being moved out of the quarry.

Portland stone industry, August 1966. The quarryman is driving in plugs and feathers to split the stone.

Stone quarry block which has been split with plugs and feathers, 1966. The Portland stone tradition continues to the present day. In 1972 approximately 600 tons were quarried for the restoration of St Paul's Cathedral, and in 1990 Portland stone was used for the carved façade of the Sainsbury extension to the National Gallery.

Here we see a quarryman in one of the Grove quarries, shaping a block of stone with a big kivel, summer 1966. There are plugs and feathers on top of the blocks.

A quarryman in Portland Stone Quarry removing plugs and feathers, summer 1966.

Portland Stone Quarry, summer 1966. Here we see a quarryman using a pneumatic drill to make holes for feather and plugs.

The unveiling of the Cenotaph in Whitehall by King George V, November 1920, was attended by thousands of people. On that grey November day the noble lines of the Cenotaph became the focal point of the nation's pride and grief. Few realized that the stone used for the Cenotaph came from Portland, and the carefully selected stone was first shaped with tools such as the small and large kivels pictured here.

A delightful photograph of the Portland Saunders standing outside their house at Mallams, *c.* 1900. Standing on the left is Rose Ann Saunders.

This photograph of the Saunders family gives a strong impression of the personalities of the Saunders parents, William, who died in July 1904, aged 75, and his wife Rose Ann, who died on 6 September 1914, aged 78.

The back of this photograph, taken in 1938 by Wyndham Goodden of Upwey, is simply captioned 'Portland men'. Although from their appearance they were probably fishermen no details of the occasion or subjects are known, so any information from readers would be appreciated.

The Observatory, Portland, 1899. The man on the left is possibly the Revd W.R. Waugh.

General view of Portland and Sandsfoot Castle, 1890. The ruins of Sandsfoot Castle pictured here were a popular haunt of holiday-makers during the second half of the nineteenth century.

Acknowledgements

I am grateful to those who have helped in the compilation of this book by contributing valuable information. Thanks must go to Arthur Chapple, Edna Everitt and Miss Kathleen Deacon who gave much-appreciated assistance. I am grateful to my wife Carol for her encouragement and help. Thanks must also go to Simon Fletcher of Alan Sutton Publishing Ltd for his assistance.

The photographs in this book all come from the wonderful collection in the photographic record department of the Dorset County Museum. I am indebted to Richard de Peyer, the curator, for allowing these pictures to be used and for the kindness and help shown to me by Miss Val Dicker who made the task of putting together this book a pleasure.

Old photographs are truly fascinating. They bring back so vividly times past, and to live in them is never to die. To the young the past must seem like a foreign land, but the generation born before the Second World War recognize its beauty and are left with a haunting sense of loss.

BRITAIN IN OLD PHOTOGRAPHS

To order any of these titles please telephone Littlehampton Book Services on 01903 721596

ALDERNEY

Alderney: A Second Selection, *B Bonnard*

BEDFORDSHIRE

Bedfordshire at Work, *N Lutt*

BERKSHIRE

Maidenhead, *M Hayles & D Hedges*
Around Maidenhead, *M Hayles & B Hedges*
Reading, *P Southerton*
Reading: A Second Selection, *P Southerton*
Sandhurst and Crowthorne, *K Dancy*
Around Slough, *J Hunter & K Hunter*
Around Thatcham, *P Allen*
Around Windsor, *B Hedges*

BUCKINGHAMSHIRE

Buckingham and District, *R Cook*
High Wycombe, *R Goodearl*
Around Stony Stratford, *A Lambert*

CHESHIRE

Cheshire Railways, *M Hitches*
Chester, *S Nichols*

CLWYD

Clwyd Railways, *M Hitches*

CLYDESDALE

Clydesdale, *Lesmahagow Parish Historical Association*

CORNWALL

Cornish Coast, *T Bowden*
Falmouth, *P Gilson*
Lower Fal, *P Gilson*
Around Padstow, *M McCarthy*
Around Penzance, *J Holmes*
Penzance and Newlyn, *J Holmes*
Around Truro, *A Lyne*
Upper Fal, *P Gilson*

CUMBERLAND

Cockermouth and District, *J Bernard Bradbury*
Keswick and the Central Lakes, *J Marsh*
Around Penrith, *F Boyd*
Around Whitehaven, *H Fancy*

DERBYSHIRE

Derby, *D Buxton*
Around Matlock, *D Barton*

DEVON

Colyton and Seaton, *T Gosling*
Dawlish and Teignmouth, *G Gosling*
Devon Aerodromes, *K Saunders*
Exeter, *P Thomas*
Exmouth and Budleigh Salterton, *T Gosling*
From Haldon to Mid-Dartmoor, *T Hall*
Honiton and the Otter Valley, *J Yallop*
Around Kingsbridge, *K Tanner*
Around Seaton and Sidmouth, *T Gosling*
Seaton, Axminster and Lyme Regis, *T Gosling*

DORSET

Around Blandford Forum, *B Cox*
Bournemouth, *M Colman*
Bridport and the Bride Valley, *J Burrell & S Humphries*
Dorchester, *T Gosling*
Around Gillingham, *P Crocker*

DURHAM

Darlington, *G Flynn*
Darlington: A Second Selection, *G Flynn*
Durham People, *M Richardson*
Houghton-le-Spring and Hetton-le-Hole, *K Richardson*
Houghton-le-Spring and Hetton-le-Hole:
   A Second Selection, *K Richardson*
Sunderland, *S Miller & B Bell*
Teesdale, *D Coggins*
Teesdale: A Second Selection, *P Raine*
Weardale, *J Crosby*
Weardale: A Second Selection, *J Crosby*

DYFED

Aberystwyth and North Ceredigion,
   Dyfed Cultural Services Dept
Haverfordwest, *Dyfed Cultural Services Dept*
Upper Tywi Valley, *Dyfed Cultural Services Dept*

ESSEX

Around Grays, *B Evans*

GLOUCESTERSHIRE

Along the Avon from Stratford to Tewkesbury, *J Jeremiah*
Cheltenham: A Second Selection, *R Whiting*
Cheltenham at War, *P Gill*
Cirencester, *J Welsford*
Around Cirencester, *E Cuss & P Griffiths*
Forest, The, *D Mullin*
Gloucester, *J Voyce*
Around Gloucester, *A Sutton*
Gloucester: From the Walwin Collection, *J Voyce*
North Cotswolds, *D Viner*
Severn Vale, *A Sutton*
Stonehouse to Painswick, *A Sutton*
Stroud and the Five Valleys, *S Gardiner & L Padin*
Stroud and the Five Valleys: A Second Selection,
   S Gardiner & L Padin
Stroud's Golden Valley, *S Gardiner & L Padin*
Stroudwater and Thames & Severn Canals,
   E Cuss & S Gardiner
Stroudwater and Thames & Severn Canals: A Second
   Selection, *E Cuss & S Gardiner*
Tewkesbury and the Vale of Gloucester, *C Hilton*
Thornbury to Berkeley, *J Hudson*
Uley, Dursley and Cam, *A Sutton*
Wotton-under-Edge to Chipping Sodbury, *A Sutton*

GWYNEDD

Anglesey, *M Hitches*
Gwynedd Railways, *M Hitches*
Around Llandudno, *M Hitches*
Vale of Conwy, *M Hitches*

HAMPSHIRE

Gosport, *J Sadden*
Portsmouth, *P Rogers & D Francis*

HEREFORDSHIRE

Herefordshire, *A Sandford*

HERTFORDSHIRE

Barnet, *I Norrie*
Hitchin, *A Fleck*
St Albans, *S Mullins*
Stevenage, *M Appleton*

ISLE OF MAN

The Tourist Trophy, *B Snelling*

ISLE OF WIGHT

Newport, *D Parr*
Around Ryde, *D Parr*

JERSEY

Jersey: A Third Selection, *R Lemprière*

KENT

Bexley, *M Scott*
Broadstairs and St Peter's, *J Whyman*
Bromley, Keston and Hayes, *M Scott*
Canterbury: A Second Selection, *D Butler*
Chatham and Gillingham, *P MacDougall*
Chatham Dockyard, *P MacDougall*
Deal, *J Broady*
Early Broadstairs and St Peter's, *B Wootton*
East Kent at War, *D Collyer*
Eltham, *J Kennett*
Folkestone: A Second Selection, *A Taylor & E Rooney*
Goudhurst to Tenterden, *A Guilmant*
Gravesend, *R Hiscock*
Around Gravesham, *R Hiscock & D Grierson*
Herne Bay, *J Hawkins*
Lympne Airport, *D Collyer*
Maidstone, *I Hales*
Margate, *R Clements*
RAF Hawkinge, *R Humphreys*
RAF Manston, *RAF Manston History Club*
RAF Manston: A Second Selection,
   RAF Manston History Club
Ramsgate and Thanet Life, *D Perkins*
Romney Marsh, *E Carpenter*
Sandwich, *C Wanostrocht*
Around Tonbridge, *C Bell*
Tunbridge Wells, *M Rowlands & I Beavis*
Tunbridge Wells: A Second Selection,
   M Rowlands & I Beavis
Around Whitstable, *C Court*
Wingham, Adisham and Littlebourne, *M Crane*

LANCASHIRE

Around Barrow-in-Furness, *J Garbutt & J Marsh*
Blackpool, *C Rothwell*
Bury, *J Hudson*
Chorley and District, *J Smith*
Fleetwood, *C Rothwell*
Heywood, *J Hudson*
Around Kirkham, *C Rothwell*
Lancashire North of the Sands, *J Garbutt & J Marsh*
Around Lancaster, *S Ashworth*
Lytham St Anne's, *C Rothwell*
North Fylde, *C Rothwell*
Radcliffe, *J Hudson*
Rossendale, *B Moore & N Dunnachie*

LEICESTERSHIRE

Around Ashby-de-la-Zouch, *K Hillier*
Charnwood Forest, *I Keil, W Humphrey & D Wix*
Leicester, *D Burton*
Leicester: A Second Selection, *D Burton*
Melton Mowbray, *T Hickman*
Around Melton Mowbray, *T Hickman*
River Soar, *D Wix, P Shacklock & I Keil*
Rutland, *T Clough*
Vale of Belvoir, *T Hickman*
Around the Welland Valley, *S Mastoris*

LINCOLNSHIRE

Grimsby, *J Tierney*
Around Grimsby, *J Tierney*
Grimsby Docks, *J Tierney*
Lincoln, *D Cuppleditch*